the ScumMage

Nicholas Halliday

www.scuMMage.com

For Lily, the original Scummage ...

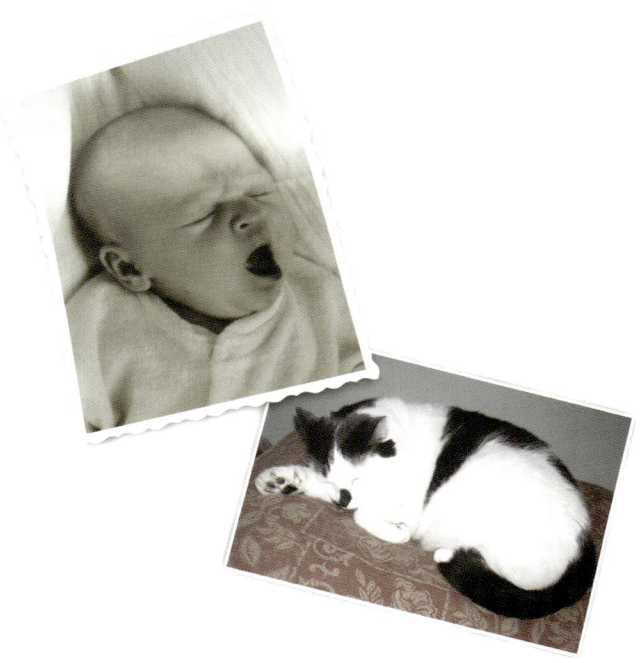

... and Elgar, the fat lazy cat we love.

A strange new pet has got everyone fussing.
I'm not allowed near it and that keeps me guessing.
I've called it the Scummage, but I'm not quite sure,
as I've never known anything like it before.

Since it's been in the house it's wanted to eat,
but the food's in its hair, on its face and its feet!
Scummage threw some at me.
"That's not funny!" said mummy.

Could it be a messy pig
with a big round tummy?

When the Scummage stops eating I try to be friends,
but smelly stuff keeps coming out of both ends.
They keep cleaning up but it keeps coming out.

Could there be a slimy
green Martian about?

Sometimes the Scummage knows how to behave
and most of the day it just sleeps in its cage.
What cunning beast waits for night 'till it pounces?

Could it be a sly fox,
nine pounds and two ounces?

I'm tired all the time but it knows when I'm sleeping.
If I'm tucked up in bed Scummage wakes me by screaming.
What is it that makes this nocturnal din?

Could it be a mad owl
learning the violin?

Now the Scummage is growing it's started to chew.
If it fits in its mouth is on the menu.
There aren't many teeth but they're sharp as can be.

Could it be a shark
from the deep blue sea?

It cries through the night, chews its toys and it's smelly.
It sleeps all day long after filling its tummy,

but I love the Scummage and the Scummage loves me.
It's not monstrous at all it's a sweet little …

... baby!

Written, scummaged and illustrated by Nicholas Halliday

This edition first published 2007 by HallidayBooks

www.hallidaybooks.com · www.scummage.com · info@hallidaybooks.com

ISBN 978-0-9539459-1-7

The Owl and the Pussycat original words by Edward Lear, 1871
Original music score by Igor Stravinsky, 1966

Mars landscape © NASA

Printed and bound in Spain by Estudios Gráficos ZURE S.A.

HALLIDAYBOOKS
www.hallidaybooks.com

Nicholas with daughter Lily

The Author

Nicholas Halliday studied at Epsom School of Art and Design, Lancashire Polytechnic and Kingston Polytechnic. Since graduating from Kingston in 1991 with a BA in graphic design, he has worked as a designer and illustrator. He now runs HallidayBooks publishing original children's titles. He has a daughter Lily, to whom *The Scummage* is dedicated.

Acknowledgments

Thanks go to my mother Jennifer, for her constant support and encouragement and to Sandra Smith who's kind and generous actions have helped me more than she knows. Sincere thanks also goes to Anders and Sue for feeding my mind, body and soul over the last few years.

My love and gratitude go to my beautiful daughter Lily for her honest and insightful wisdom and for letting me know what's funny and what's not. Lily is the original Scummage, the inspiration for this book and a constant inspiration for my life. Thanks angel girl.

The Lonely Tree
NICHOLAS HALLIDAY

This beautiful and moving story follows the first year in the life of a lone evergreen tree growing in the heart of the ancient oak woodland of the New Forest. The evergreen is befriended by the oldest oak who has lived for hundreds of years. When winter arrives all the oak trees must go to sleep, but of course evergreens never sleep. Finally, after a long, cold and lonely winter, spring brings both sadness and joy to the little tree.

Join the old oak, the barn owl, the ponies and the squirrels in this enchanting, universally praised, life affirming tale.

'Utterly, completely and splendidly charming. Originally illustrated and delightfully told.'
Stephen Fry

'Compelling! This book has something very special about it.'
The Observer

'Really lovely ... really beautiful ... really wonderful!'
ITV News

Richly illustrated and sympathetically explored for younger readers and, of course, that last acorn is the seed for a happy ending.
Times Education Suppliment

'Unusual and enchanting. The trees are the heroes: the illustrations are full of secrets: the message is love.'
Joanna Lumley

'A picture book that will appeal to the whole family.'
Children's Books UK

Paperback ISBN: 978-09539459-8-6 • Hardback ISBN: 978-09539459-6-2

Available in all good bookshops and at www.hallidaybooks.com